smoothies&juices

a selection of refreshing and invigorating drinks

p

This is a Parragon Book
This edition published in 2007

Parragon
Queen Street House
4 Queen Street
Bath, BA1 1HE

ISBN: 978-1-4054-8762-7

Printed in China

This edition designed by Emily Wilkinson
Cover design by Talking Design
Front cover photography by Günter Beer
Back cover photography by Karen Thomas

Notes for the Reader

This book uses both metric and imperial
measurements. Follow the same units of
measurement throughout; do not mix metric
and imperial.

All spoon measurements are level; teaspoons
are assumed to be 15ml.

Unless otherwise stated, milk is assumed to be
full fat, individual vegetables such as potatoes
are medium, and pepper is freshly ground
black pepper.

Recipes using raw or very lightly cooked eggs
should be avoided by infants, the elderly,
pregnant women, convalescents and anyone
suffering from an illness. Pregnant and
breastfeeding women are advised to avoid
eating peanuts and peanut products.

The times given are an approximate guide only.
Preparation times differ according to the
techniques used by different people and the
cooking times may also vary from those given.

contents

introduction

There is such an array of exotic fruits available today, and blending them into a delicious smoothie or using them for innovative juices is an excellent way to enjoy them all year round.

We are all more health-conscious than we used to be, and are more informed about artificial additives, sugar, sweeteners and preservatives in our food. Some commercial drinks may look healthy enough, but a closer look at the label will reveal that they contain a number of chemicals we would rather do without. These drinks can be rather too sweet, or bland and unappetising. It makes sense, therefore, to blend your own fruit and vegetable drinks. This way, you can be sure that what you are drinking contains no hidden additives and you can also opt for organic raw ingredients. Once you get into the habit of making your own drinks, you will find yourself buying commercial varieties less and less.

We are encouraged to eat about five portions of fresh fruit and vegetables a day, but our modern hectic lifestyle means this is often impossible. Consuming them in drink form is a quick, easy and agreeable way to ensure we keep to this target and receive the recommended daily amount of vitamins we need. You can devise your own smoothie and juice recipes, based on your favourite ingredients, but the rule is that it is usually best not to combine fruit and vegetables in any one drink. Exceptions to this rule are apples, carrots and tomatoes, which blend happily with most other ingredients.

If you are going to be creating your own drinks recipes on a regular basis, it makes sense to keep a well-stocked fruit bowl at all times, with apples, oranges, grapes and other fruit. Do not be afraid to experiment with fruit that may be unfamiliar to you, such as pomegranates, watermelon or guavas, as they make delicious and refreshingly palate-cleansing drinks. You will also find it a good idea to keep a generous supply of frozen fruit in the freezer at all times, such as bananas, strawberries, blackberries and peaches. Use them straight from the freezer to make a refreshing, chilled drink at any time of the year.

Whenever you have a surplus of fruit, freeze some away for future use in drinks and then you can enjoy your favourite fruit even when it is out of season. Freeze banana slices in a single layer on a tray, then transfer them to freezer bags. You can do the same with small chunks or slices of other fruits. Combined with your favourite ice cream or sorbet, they can be turned into mouthwatering drinks at the drop of a hat. Keep lots of ice cubes in the freezer, too, and a plentiful supply of mineral water, milk and yogurt in the fridge.

equipment

You do not need a wide range of fancy or expensive equipment to make your own drinks. Some basic utensils will do the job perfectly well. For the best results, use a food processor and a juicer.

A standard food processor can produce a smoothie in a matter of seconds with no trouble at all. If you do not have a food processor, you can use a blender for many of the recipes, but it should be a fairly resilient model.

Unlike a food processor, which turns ingredients into a purée, a juicer separates the juice from the pulp of a fruit. Juicers vary in price and performance and range from the more inexpensive centrifugal ones, which extract the juice by means of centrifugal force, to the more expensive hydraulic varieties, which may seem an extravagance but produce really excellent results by retaining plenty of nutrients. Triturating juicers are in the middle of both the price and nutritional range. The hydraulic type is best because the juice is forced out through extreme pressure, retaining all the essential nutrients, and so, if you are a great natural juice fan, this is the obvious choice for you.

Consider also the size of a juicer before you invest in one, especially if your kitchen space is limited. Triturating juicers are larger than the other varieties. Other factors to take into account are the speed at which they produce juice and whether they are easy or fiddly to clean.

You will already have any other equipment needed for making drinks in your kitchen cupboards and drawers, such as sharp knives, chopping boards, ice-cube trays and freezer bags.

techniques

You do not have to be a great expert to make your own smoothies and juices, but it helps to bear a few tips in mind.

Wash, peel and prepare fruit and vegetables thoroughly because everything you put into the food processor bowl or blender goblet will end up as part of the final drink. Remember to remove stones, pips and seeds as required. Smaller seeds and pips such as those found in grapes, apples and pears, can stay. Chop larger fruit and vegetables such as apples or carrots, into manageable chunks.

Crush ice cubes before you add them to the food processor, or you will damage the sharp blade. To do this, place them between two clean tea towels and hammer them with a rolling pin.

With juicers, you do not need to peel most fruit and vegetables, except for tough-skinned varieties such as bananas, kiwi fruit and citrus fruit, but you should always wash them thoroughly first. More heavy-duty juicers can cope with tough skins, such as melon skin, but check the manufacturer's instructions carefully before taking a risk. Many of the essential nutrients in fruit and vegetables are found just close to the skin, so it can be important to retain it during juicing for maximum health benefits. Always remember to use fresh and unblemished fruit and vegetables.

Enjoy making up your own drinks recipes, whether a juice, smoothie, slush, float or milkshake. Be bold and imaginative in your flavour and colour combinations. Devising your own drinks is healthy, easy and, above all, great fun.

fresh & fruity

an abundance of bright colours, sweet pleasures and sour delights await you in this chapter. By freezing fruit while in season you can enjoy nature's gifts throughout the year. A host of treats lie ahead, including a forest fruit smoothie or a kiwi cooler.

white grape & elderflower

Use champagne or muscat grapes to add to the delicate floweriness of this light smoothie.

SERVES 2

**125 g/4¹/₂ oz white grapes,
deseeded or seedless
200 ml/7 fl oz sparkling
mineral water
2 large scoops of
frozen yogurt (plain)
1¹/₂ tbsp elderflower cordial**

Put the grapes, mineral water, frozen yogurt and elderflower cordial in a food processor and process until smooth.

Pour into glasses and serve immediately.

apricot & orange smoothie

This smoothie makes a great vitamin-and mineral-packed breakfast in a glass.

SERVES 2

250 ml/9 fl oz boiling water
125 g/4½ oz dried apricots
juice of 4 medium oranges
2 tbsp natural yogurt
1 tsp soft dark brown sugar

Put the apricots in a bowl and pour the boiling water over them. Leave to soak overnight.

In the morning, put the apricots and their soaking water into a food processor and process until puréed. Add the orange juice to the apricots in the food processor, and process until combined.

Pour into glasses and top with 1 tablespoon of yogurt and a sprinkling of brown sugar.

kiwi cooler

Use a **strawberry ice cream** to contrast with the glorious green colour of this **smoothie**, or a lime sorbet to tone in with it. **Whichever** you choose, the **combination** will be **delightful**.

SERVES 2

**4 ripe kiwi fruit,
peeled and quartered
200 ml/7 fl oz traditional
sparkling lemonade
2 large scoops of ice cream
or sorbet**

Put the kiwi fruit and lemonade into a food processor and process until smooth.

Pour into glasses and top with a scoop of ice cream or sorbet.

Serve at once.

ruby anyday

Too good just for tuesdays, this is ruby anyday.

SERVES 2

1 large ripe pink or ruby grapefruit
100 ml/3¹/₂ fl oz ice-cold water
100 g/3¹/₂ oz Greek yogurt
1 tbsp flowery clear honey,
such as acacia

Quarter the grapefruit, then pull off the peel and as much pith as possible. Discard any seeds.

Put the grapefruit and water into a food processor and process until smooth. Add the yogurt and honey and process again until combined.

Pour into glasses and serve at once.

melon refresher

Incorporating three different types of melons, the flavour of this smoothie is both delicate and refreshing on a hot day.

SERVES 2

250 ml/9 fl oz natural yogurt
100 g/3$\frac{1}{2}$ oz galia melon,
cut into chunks
100 g/3$\frac{1}{2}$ oz cantaloupe melon,
cut into chunks
100 g/3$\frac{1}{2}$ oz watermelon,
cut into chunks
6 ice cubes

DECORATION
wedges of melon

Pour the yogurt into a food processor. Add the galia melon chunks and process until smooth.

Add the cantaloupe and watermelon chunks along with the ice cubes and process until smooth.

Pour the mixture into glasses and decorate with wedges of melon.

Serve at once.

papaya sweet & sour

Papaya undergoes an amazing transformation as it ripens. With the outside skin yellow, the soft ripe papaya is a deep sunset pink inside. Unripe, the dark green rind can be peeled away to reveal the crisp light green, tart fruit with a texture similar to that of an apple.

SERVES 2

250 g/8 oz ripe soft papaya
200 ml/7 fl oz ice-cold water
juice of 1 lime

DECORATION
slices of green papaya

Peel the ripe papaya, discarding any seeds. Cut into chunks.

Put the papaya chunks into a food processor with the water and lime and process until smooth.

Pour into glasses and decorate with slices of green papaya.

blueberry thrill

Blueberries are still a much underrated pleasure. In this smoothie their raw, tart sweetness is enhanced by the yogurt.

SERVES 2

100 ml/3¹/₂ fl oz Greek yogurt
100 ml/3¹/₂ fl oz water
125g/4¹/₂ oz frozen blueberries

DECORATION
whole frozen blueberries

Put the yogurt, water and blueberries into a food processor and process until smooth.

Pour into glasses and top with whole frozen blueberries.

forest fruit smoothie

This drink combines the rich flavours and colours of summer fruits in one superb smoothie.

SERVES 2

350 ml/12 fl oz orange juice
1 banana, sliced and frozen
450 g/1 lb frozen forest fruits
(such as blueberries, raspberries
and blackberries)

DECORATION
slices of fresh strawberry

Pour the orange juice into a food processor. Add the banana and half of the forest fruits and process until smooth.

Add the remaining forest fruits and process until smooth. Pour the mixture into tall glasses and decorate the rims with slices of fresh strawberry.

Add straws and serve.

green gala

Set off the beautiful **green colour of** this **smoothie** by placing a **strawberry** or two on the **rim** of the **glass.**

SERVES 2

**2 ripe kiwi fruit,
peeled and quartered
200 g/7 oz frozen galia melon balls
2 scoops lemon sorbet
2 tbsp water**

**DECORATION
strawberries**

Put the kiwi fruit, melon balls, lemon sorbet and water into a food processor and process until smooth.

Pour into glasses and serve.

pear & raspberry delight

Pink, light and fruity, this refreshing smoothie is simply delicious. If you don't like the pips, you can use a sieve to make it silken smooth.

SERVES 2

2 large ripe conference pears
125 g/4½ oz frozen raspberries
200 ml/7 fl oz ice-cold water
honey, to taste

DECORATION
raspberries on a cocktail stick

Peel and quarter the pears, removing the cores. Put into a food processor with the raspberries and water and process until smooth.

Taste and sweeten with honey if the raspberries are a little sharp.

Pour into glasses and serve.

breakfast smoothie

Kick-start your day with this rich vitamin-and mineral-packed energiser.

SERVES 2

250 ml/9 fl oz orange juice
125 ml/4 fl oz natural yogurt
2 eggs
2 bananas, sliced and frozen

DECORATION
slice of fresh banana

Pour the orange juice and yogurt into a food processor and process gently until combined.

Add the eggs and frozen bananas and process until smooth.

Pour the mixture into glasses and decorate the rims with a slice of fresh banana.

Add straws and serve.

orange & strawberry cream

The **impeccable** combination of fresh **flavours** makes this **one** of the **most** popular **smoothies.**

SERVES 2

125 ml/4 fl oz natural yogurt
175 ml/6 fl oz strawberry yogurt
175 ml/6 fl oz orange juice
175 g/6 oz frozen strawberries
1 banana, sliced and frozen

DECORATION
slice of orange
whole fresh strawberry

Pour the natural and strawberry yogurts into a food processor and process gently. Add the orange juice and process until combined.

Add the strawberries and banana and process until smooth.

Pour the mixture into tall glasses and decorate with slices of orange and whole strawberries.

Add straws and serve.

gooseberry foolish

It is foolish indeed to ignore gooseberries. Ripe and fragrant, they have a rich, fruitiness that combines brilliantly with custard-style yogurt. Dessert gooseberries are not small and green but large and a deep plummy red.

SERVES 2

250 g/9 oz ripe dessert gooseberries
200 ml/7 fl oz water
2–4 tbsp golden granulated sugar
200 ml/7 fl oz custard-style
vanilla yogurt

DECORATION
a few flaked almonds

Put the gooseberries, water and sugar into a small saucepan. Cover tightly, place over a medium heat and simmer for about 15 minutes, or until the gooseberries have split and are very soft. Allow to cool.

Put the gooseberries and their cooking liquid into a food processor and process until smooth. Add the yogurt and process again until combined.

Pour into glasses and sprinkle with flaked almonds to serve.

mango & orange smoothie

If you want a creamy smoothie, use vanilla ice cream instead of mango sorbet. The mango must be quite ripe and fragrant. It should be soft and yield to gentle pressure.

SERVES 2

1 large ripe mango
juice of 2 medium oranges
3 scoops of mango sorbet

DECORATION
1 strip of orange zest

Place the mango on a chopping board and cut lengthways through the flesh as close to the large flat central stone as possible. Turn it over and do the same thing on the other side of the stone. Remove the peel and roughly chop the flesh before placing in a processor.

Add the orange juice and sorbet and process until smooth.

Serve at once, decorated with a strip of orange zest if liked.

green tea & yellow plum

The haunting flavour of green tea combines brilliantly with golden-yellow plums. If the weather isn't wonderful, this smoothie is just as delicious served warm.

SERVES 2

1 green tea with oriental spice tea bag
300 ml/10 fl oz boiling water
1 tbsp sugar
125 g/4½ oz ripe yellow plums, halved and stoned

Put the tea bag in a teapot or jug and pour over the boiling water. Leave to infuse for 7 minutes. Remove and discard the tea bag. Allow to cool, then chill.

Pour the chilled tea into a food processor. Add the sugar and plums and process until smooth.

Serve at once.

cherry sour

Use the **bottling liquid** as well as the **fruit** for this **sharp,** thirst-quenching **smoothie.**

SERVES 2

250 g/9 oz bottled morello cherries
150 ml/5 fl oz Greek yogurt
sugar, to taste
almond thins, to serve

DECORATION
cherries on a cocktail stick

Put the cherries with their bottling liquid into a food processor with the yogurt and process until smooth.

Taste and sweeten with sugar if necessary.

Pour into glasses and serve with almond thins.

strawberry surprise

This supremely thirst-quenching smoothie is ideal to serve on scorching summer days. The balsamic vinegar brings out the flavour of the strawberries beautifully.

SERVES 2

125 g/4½ oz frozen strawberries
200 ml/7 fl oz ice-cold water
1 tbsp balsamic vinegar
1 tbsp flowery clear honey,
such as acacia

DECORATION
2 fresh mint sprigs

Put the strawberries, water, balsamic vinegar and honey in a food processor and process until smooth.

Pour into glasses and serve decorated with the mint.

honeydew

The natural texture of the honeydew melon lends itself to this delicate smoothie. For best results, make sure the melon is truly ripe.

SERVES 2

250 g/9 oz honeydew melon
300 ml/10 fl oz sparkling
mineral water
2 tbsp clear honey

DECORATION
redcurrant clusters

Cut the rind off the melon. Chop the melon into chunks, discarding any seeds.

Put into a food processor with the water and honey and process until smooth.

Pour into glasses and decorate with a slice of strawberry or a cluster of redcurrants to set off the pale yellow.

fig & maple melter

Go on, indulge yourself in this rich, delicious and sophisticated smoothie.

SERVES 2

350 ml/12 fl oz hazelnut yogurt
2 tbsp freshly squeezed
orange juice
4 tbsp maple syrup
8 large fresh figs, chopped
6 ice cubes

DECORATION
toasted chopped hazelnuts

Pour the yogurt, orange juice and maple syrup into a food processor and process gently until combined.

Add the figs and ice cubes and process until smooth.

Pour the mixture into glasses and scatter over some toasted chopped hazelnuts.

Serve at once.

blackcurrant bracer

Purple passion! For a strictly grown-up version, use crème de cassis instead of the cordial.

SERVES 2

100 g/3½ oz frozen blackcurrants
4 scoops of blackcurrant sorbet
100 ml/3½ fl oz crème fraîche
2 tbsp blackcurrant cordial,
plus extra for drizzling
1 tbsp water
sugar, to taste

DECORATION
a few mint leaves

Put the blackcurrants, sorbet, crème fraîche, cordial and water into a food processor and process until smooth. Taste and sweeten with a little sugar if necessary.

Pour into glasses. Drizzle over some cordial, decorate with the mint leaves and serve.

peach & cinnamon layer

Serve this in tall thin glasses to make the most of its layers.

Mix the sugar and breadcrumbs together and spread the mixture out on a baking sheet. Place under a moderate grill or in a hot oven (200°C, 400°F, Gas Mark 6) for about 7–10 minutes. Watch the crumbs carefully and turn frequently until they are nicely browned. Add the cinnamon and mix well. Allow to cool.

Pour boiling water over the peaches to scald them. Drain, then peel and quarter them, discarding the stones. Put into a food processor and process until smooth. Set aside and wash the food processor bowl. Put the milk and ice cream into the food processor and blend until combined.

Pour a little of the milk and ice-cream mixture into each glass, spoon over some peach purée and sprinkle over a few cinnamon breadcrumbs. Carefully repeat these layers until you reach the top of the glass. Serve at once.

SERVES 2

2 tbsp soft dark brown sugar
2 tbsp soft brown breadcrumbs
1 tsp ground cinnamon
4 ripe peaches
150 ml/5 fl oz milk
3 large scoops of luxury vanilla ice cream

DECORATION
sugar and breadcrumbs

peach and redcurrant sunset

Make sure the peaches you use are properly ripe so their flavour counteracts the acidity of the redcurrants. This classic combination of flavours makes a very pretty smoothie. Run the prongs of a fork along each redcurrant stalk to release the redcurrants.

SERVES 2

2 large ripe peaches
100 g/3½ oz redcurrants
200 ml/7 fl oz ice-cold water
1–2 tbsp clear honey

Halve the peaches and discard the stones. Roughly chop and put into the food processor.

Keep 2 stems of redcurrants whole for decoration and strip the rest off their stalks into a food processor. Add the water and honey and process until smooth.

Pour into glasses and decorate with the remaining redcurrant sprigs.

apple cooler

The distinctive flavour of fragrant, ripe apples combines with fresh strawberries and freshly squeezed orange juice to give you a really zingy smoothie.

SERVES 2

2 ripe apples, peeled and roughly chopped
55 g/2 oz strawberries, hulled
juice of 4 oranges
sugar, to taste

Put the apples, strawberries and orange juice into a food processor and process until smooth.

Taste and sweeten with sugar if necessary.

Serve at once.

raw & revitalising

nature's bounty provides us with delicious and healthy drinks, packed with energy and vitality. Try a nourishing carrot and ginger energiser or a pomegranate passion for the wonderful feeling of wellbeing.

blood orange sparkler

Now that **blood** (ruby) **orange juice** is **available** all year **round, you can** use its **fabulous** colour and **flavour** whenever **you** want.

SERVES 2

250 ml/9 fl oz blood (ruby) orange juice
100 g/3½ oz strawberries
100 g/3½ oz raspberries
50 ml/2 fl oz sparkling mineral water

Put the blood orange juice, strawberries, raspberries and mineral water into a food processor and process until smooth. Sieve the mixture to remove the pips, if preferred.

Pour into glasses and serve.

tomato blazer

Tangy and a little bit hot, this is a juice with a bit of get-up-and-go!

SERVES 2

500 ml/18 fl oz tomato juice
dash of Worcestershire sauce
1 small red chilli, deseeded
and chopped
1 spring onion, trimmed
 and chopped
6 ice cubes

DECORATION
2 long, thin red chillies,
cut into flowers

To make the chilli flowers, use a sharp knife to make six cuts along each chilli. Place the point of the knife about 1 cm/$1/2$ inch from the stalk end and cut towards the tip. Put the chillies in a bowl of iced water and leave them for 25–30 minutes, or until they have spread out into flower shapes.

Put the tomato juice and Worcestershire sauce into a food processor and process gently until combined. Add the chopped chilli, spring onion and ice cubes and process until smooth.

Pour the mixture into glasses and garnish with the chilli flowers.

Add straws and serve.

carrot & pepper booster

This dynamic combination of flavours will fire up your system and boost your energy levels.

SERVES 2

250 ml/9 fl oz carrot juice
250 ml/9 fl oz tomato juice
2 large red peppers, deseeded
and roughly chopped
1 tbsp lemon juice
freshly ground black pepper

Pour the carrot juice and tomato juice into a food processor and process gently until combined.

Add the red peppers and lemon juice. Season with plenty of freshly ground black pepper and process until smooth.

Pour the mixture into tall glasses, add straws and serve.

carrot cream

Carrots have a strong hint of sweetness that makes them and their juice an excellent and delicious base for mixed drinks.

SERVES 2

150 ml/5 fl oz carrot juice
90 ml/3 fl oz single cream
15 ml/1 fl oz orange juice
1 egg yolk
4 cracked ice cubes
1 slice of orange

Pour the carrot juice, cream and orange juice over ice in a shaker and add the egg yolk.

Shake vigorously until well mixed.

Strain into chilled glasses and decorate with the orange slice.

pom pom

Lemonade is transformed into an extravaganza that's pretty in pink, with a frothy topping to match its frivolous name.

SERVES 2

juice of 1 lemon
2 egg whites
1 tsp grenadine
150 ml/5 fl oz lemonade
crushed ice
slice of lemon

Blend the lemon juice, egg whites and grenadine together in a food processor and pour into glasses filled with crushed ice.

Top up with lemonade and dress with a slice of lemon.

strawberry & pineapple refresher

Long-life pineapple juice and frozen fruit are used in this easy-to-assemble store cupboard treat – the flavours are not compromised by your haste!

SERVES 2

150 g/5½ oz frozen strawberries
300 ml/10 fl oz long-life pineapple juice
1 tbsp caster sugar

Put the strawberries, pineapple juice and caster sugar into a food processor and blend until smooth.

Serve at once.

black grape fizz

Use large dark grapes for this foamy, refreshing cooler.

SERVES 2

**25 g/4¹/₂ oz black grapes, deseeded or seedless
200 ml/7 fl oz sparkling mineral water
2 large scoops of lemon sorbet**

Put the grapes, mineral water and lemon sorbet in a food processor and process until smooth.

Pour into glasses and serve immediately.

homemade lemonade

This classic cooler is a well-loved, traditional favourite.

Put the water, sugar and grated lemon rind into a small saucepan and bring to the boil, stirring constantly. Continue to boil, stirring, for 5 minutes.

Remove from the heat and leave to cool to room temperature. Stir in the lemon juice, then transfer to a jug, cover with clingfilm and chill in the refrigerator for at least 2 hours.

When the lemonade has almost finished chilling, take two glasses and rub the rims with a wedge of lemon, then dip them in granulated sugar to frost. Put the ice cubes into the glasses.

Remove the lemon syrup from the refrigerator, pour it over the ice and top up with sparkling water. The ratio should be one part lemon syrup to three parts sparkling water. Stir well to mix, decorate with sugar and slices of fresh lemon and serve.

SERVES 2

150 ml/5 fl oz water
6 tbsp sugar
1 tsp grated lemon rind
125 ml/4 fl oz lemon juice
6 ice cubes
sparkling water, to serve

DECORATION
granulated sugar
slices of lemon

watermelon whizz

A great favourite in Greece, where roadside stalls sell enormous watermelons, this thirst quencher makes the most of this gigantic fruit's juiciness.

SERVES 2

1 wedge of watermelon,
weighing about 350 g/12 oz
ice cubes

DECORATION
1–2 fresh mint sprigs

Cut the rind off the watermelon. Chop the watermelon into chunks, discarding any seeds.

Put the watermelon chunks into a food processor and process until smooth.

Place ice cubes in the glasses. Pour the watermelon mixture over the ice and serve decorated with the mint.

wake up sweetie

Wake up sweetie, or even ugli, depending on how you feel. Sweetie grapefruit and ugli fruit are very similar – a hybrid of grapefruit, they are sweeter and juicier, perfect to wake you up in the morning.

SERVES 2

**3 large ripe sweetie grapefruit
or ugli fruit
150ml/5 fl oz sparkling water
1 tbsp flowery runny honey (optional)
some slices of lime or
peeled kiwi fruit
2 tbsp low fat yogurt**

Halve and squeeze the fruit into two glasses.

Add water and honey if liked.

Serve with a slice or two of lime or kiwi, floated on the surface and topped with a spoon of yogurt.

carrot & ginger energiser

This **stimulating** blend of **flavours** is guaranteed to give you a **boost** when you **need** it.

SERVES 2

250 ml/9 fl oz carrot juice
4 tomatoes, skinned, deseeded
and roughly chopped
1 tbsp lemon juice
25 g/1 oz fresh parsley
1 tbsp grated fresh root ginger
6 ice cubes
125 ml/4 fl oz water

DECORATION
chopped fresh parsley

Put the carrot juice, tomatoes and lemon juice into a food processor and process gently until combined.

Add the parsley to the food processor along with the ginger and ice cubes. Process until well combined, then pour in the water and process until smooth.

Pour the mixture into tall glasses and garnish with chopped fresh parsley.

Serve at once.

vegetable cocktail

This savoury cocktail combines all the goodness of fresh vegetables in one glass.

SERVES 2

125 ml/4 fl oz carrot juice
500 g/1 lb 2 oz tomatoes, skinned, deseeded and roughly chopped
1 tbsp lemon juice
4 celery sticks, trimmed and sliced
4 spring onions, trimmed and roughly chopped
25 g/1 oz fresh parsley
25 g/1 oz fresh mint

DECORATION
2 celery sticks

Put the carrot juice, tomatoes and lemon juice into a food processor and process gently until combined.

Add the sliced celery along with the spring onions, parsley and mint and process until smooth.

Pour the mixture into glasses and garnish with celery sticks.

Serve at once.

spiced cranberry cordial

This looks very festive with its snowy top suspended above the spiced ruby red liquid, but it is very thirst-quenching and works well as a summer cooler.

SERVES 2

75 ml/2½ fl oz cranberry cordial
2 allspice berries, crushed
2 slices of orange
2 cinnamon sticks
250 ml/9 fl oz boiling water
2 scoops of luxury vanilla ice cream

Divide the cranberry cordial between 2 heatproof glasses, then add a crushed allspice berry, an orange slice and a cinnamon stick to each glass.

With care, pour the boiling water into the glasses. Leave to cool, then chill.

When you are ready to serve, float a scoop of ice cream on the top of each glass.

tangy apricot & apple twist

Sparkling apple juice is a great mixer, adding flavour and colour, as well as fizz. Try using it in non-alcoholic versions of cocktails such as Buck's Fizz.

SERVES 2

4 cracked ice cubes
30 ml/1 fl oz apricot juice
30 ml/1 fl oz lemon juice
90 ml/3 fl oz sparkling apple juice
twist of lemon peel

Put the cracked ice cubes into a mixing glass.

Pour the apricot juice, lemon juice and apple juice over the ice and stir well.

Strain into tall, chilled glasses and dress with a lemon twist.

grenadillo float

Grenadillos are members of the passion fruit family. They are very fragrant, with a leathery orange skin hiding the pulp and seeds.

SERVES 2

3 ripe grenadillos
250 ml/9 fl oz traditional sparkling lemonade
2 large scoops of mango sorbet
2 tsp grenadine syrup

Halve the grenadillos and scrape out the pulp and seeds into a sieve. Work the pulp through the sieve into a jug below.

Mix in the lemonade and pour into glasses.

Top with a scoop of mango sorbet and a teaspoon of grenadine syrup.

Serve.

bellini

This is a **twist** on a **classic cocktail.** Make sure the **champagne** or **moscato** di **spumante** is **thoroughly** chilled **before** you **begin.**

SERVES 2

2 large ripe peaches
300 ml/10 fl oz chilled demi-sec
champagne, Moscato di Spumante or
other sparkling white wine
(for a non-alcoholic version use
sparkling grape juice)
amaretti biscuits, to serve

Pour boiling water over the peaches to scald them. Drain, then peel and chop them, discarding the stones.

Put the chopped peaches into a food processor and process until smooth.

Divide the peach mixture between 2 champagne flutes. Stir in the champagne or sparkling wine, mixing with a swizzle stick.

Serve at once with a few amaretti biscuits.

cherry soda

Cherry soda looks very elegant and it tastes perfect too.

SERVES 2

8 ice cubes, crushed
2 tbsp cherry syrup
500 ml/18 fl oz sparkling water

DECORATION
maraschino cherries
on a cocktail stick

Divide the crushed ice between two glasses. Pour the cherry syrup over the ice.

Top up each glass with sparkling water. Decorate with the maraschino cherries on cocktail sticks and serve.

shirley temple

A classic non-alcoholic cocktail with film star appeal.

SERVES 2

sugar syrup
8 tbsp water
8 tbsp caster sugar

20 cracked ice cubes
100 ml/3½ fl oz lemon juice
15 ml/½ fl oz grenadine
ginger ale (to top up)

DECORATION
slice of orange
cocktail cherry

Make the sugar syrup by dissolving the sugar in the water over a low heat. Bring to the boil, then continue to boil without stirring for 1–2 minutes.

Put half the cracked ice cubes into a cocktail shaker. Pour the lemon juice, grenadine and sugar syrup over the ice and shake vigorously.

Half fill two small, chilled glasses with cracked ice cubes and strain the drink over them. Top up with ginger ale.

Decorate with a slice of orange and a cherry.

tonga

This is fruity, fun and a great drink to offer drivers
instead of the ubiquitous orange juice or cola!

SERVES 2

juice ½ lemon
175ml/6 fl oz pineapple juice
30ml/1 fl oz - 90ml/3 fl oz (to taste)
grapefruit juice
dash of grenadine
1 egg white
lemonade as required
slice of kiwi fruit

Shake the lemon juice, pineapple juice, grapefruit
juice, grenadine and egg white vigorously over ice.

Strain into tall glasses with a few ice cubes and
top up with lemonade.

Dress with a slice of kiwi fruit.

watercress & carrot juice

Watercress and carrot combine to make a fabulous drink that is just bursting with vitamins.

SERVES 2

500 ml/18 fl oz carrot juice
25 g/1 oz watercress
1 tbsp lemon juice
sprigs of fresh watercress, to garnish

Pour the carrot juice into a food processor. Add the watercress and lemon juice and process until smooth. Transfer to a jug, cover with clingfilm and chill in the refrigerator for at least 1 hour, or until required.

When the mixture is thoroughly chilled, pour into glasses and garnish with sprigs of fresh watercress. Serve at once.

iced citrus tea

The combination of sweet and sharp citrus flavours turns this into an irresistible drink.

SERVES 2

300 ml/10 fl oz water
2 tea bags
100 ml/3½ fl oz orange juice
4 tbsp lime juice
1–2 tbsp brown sugar
8 ice cubes

DECORATION
wedge of lime
granulated sugar
slices of orange, lemon or lime

Pour the water into a saucepan and bring to the boil. Remove from the heat, add the tea bags and leave to infuse for 5 minutes. Remove the tea bags and then leave the tea to cool to room temperature (about 30 minutes). Transfer to a jug, cover with clingfilm and chill in the refrigerator for at least 45 minutes.

When the tea has chilled, pour in the orange juice and lime juice. Add sugar to taste.

Take two glasses and rub the rims with a wedge of lime, then dip them in granulated sugar to frost. Put the ice cubes into the glasses and pour over the tea. Decorate the rims with slices of fresh orange, lemon or lime and serve.

pomegranate passion

Don't try to squeeze the pomegranate in an electric juicer, or you will make the juice bitter. This is a lovely late summer drink made with the new season's pomegranates, which start to appear in the shops in August.

SERVES 2

2 ripe pomegranates
1 passion fruit
1 tbsp clear honey
2 glasses full of crushed ice

Cut the pomegranates in half and extract the juice with an old-fashioned lemon squeezer.

Halve the passion fruit and sieve the pulp into a small bowl. Mix in the pomegranate juice and honey.

Pour over the crushed ice and serve.

raspberry & apple quencher

Quick and easy to make, this is a simple and elegant drink to enjoy.

SERVES 2

8 ice cubes, crushed
2 tbsp raspberry syrup
500 ml/18 fl oz chilled apple juice

DECORATION
whole raspberries and pieces
of apple on cocktail sticks

Divide the crushed ice between two glasses and pour over the raspberry syrup.

Top up each glass with chilled apple juice and stir well.

Decorate with the whole raspberries and pieces of apple on cocktail sticks and serve.

chilled & crushed

these drinks are the epitome of style & flair. Try a cool peppermint ice or summery berry slush and transport your imagination to sun-drenched beaches and long warm evenings.

summer fruit slush

This medley of summer berries makes an inspired drink.

SERVES 2

4 tbsp orange juice
1 tbsp lime juice
100 ml/3½ fl oz sparkling water
350 g/12 oz frozen summer fruits
(such as blueberries, raspberries,
blackberries and strawberries)
4 ice cubes

DECORATION
fresh whole raspberries and
blackberries on a cocktail stick

Pour the orange juice, lime juice and sparkling water into a food processor and process gently until combined.

Add the summer fruits and ice cubes and process until a slushy consistency has been reached.

Pour the mixture into glasses, decorate with whole raspberries and blackberries on cocktail sticks and serve.

loganberry & blackcurrant slush

Fresh, clean and simple, this is an excellent drink to serve on a really hot day. If you can't find loganberries, use a mixture of raspberries and blackberries.

SERVES 2

75 g/2³/₄ oz frozen loganberries
300 ml/10 fl oz sparkling mineral water
2 scoops of blackcurrant sorbet

Put the loganberries and water into a food processor and process until smooth.

Add the sorbet and process briefly until combined with the loganberry mixture.

Pour into glasses and drink while still slushy.

strawberry crush

This is almost a bowl of **strawberries**, so add **cream** to it as well if you like...

SERVES 2

2 egg whites
caster sugar to frost
8 oz/100g ripe strawberries
juice of 1 lemon
150ml/7fl oz lemonade, chilled
crushed ice
sugar to taste
sprig of mint

Lightly whisk the egg whites, dip the rim of the glass into it, then into the sugar and leave to dry.

Hull the strawberries and blend with the lemon, lemonade, crushed ice and sugar until smooth but frothy.

Pour into frosted glasses and finish with a sprig of mint.

cranberry & orange crush

Long and refreshing but can be quite sharp, so taste first then sweeten if necessary.

SERVES 2

juice of 4 blood oranges
250ml /8 fl oz cranberry juice
2 tbsp raspberry or other fruit syrup
sugar to taste
5 crushed ice cubes

DECORATION
raspberries

Combine together the oranges, cranberry juice and syrup juice with the crushed ice, until frothy.

Pour immediately into tall ice-filled glasses.

Serve dressed with raspberries.

the big apple

This is a fun **cocktail** to make with the **children**. Prepare several together for **convenience.**

SERVES 2

2 crisp eating apples
juice of 1 lemon
juice of 2 oranges
60ml /2 fl oz grenadine
5 crushed ice cubes

Scoop out the centre of the apples to form cup shapes, leaving the bases intact. Rub the inside with lemon juice.

Discard the cores and place the flesh in a blender, with the juices, grenadine and crushed ice.

Blend to an icy pulp and spoon back into the shells.

Drink with straws and then eat the apples!

iced coffee & chocolate slush

Coffee and a hint of peppermint combine in this delicious slush, which is topped by chocolate.

SERVES 2

400 ml/14 fl oz milk
200 ml/7 fl oz coffee syrup
100 ml/3½ fl oz peppermint syrup
1 tbsp chopped fresh mint leaves
4 ice cubes

DECORATION
grated chocolate
sprigs of fresh mint

Pour the milk, coffee syrup and peppermint syrup into a food processor and process gently until combined.

Add the mint and ice cubes and process until a slushy consistency has been reached.

Pour the mixture into glasses. Scatter over the grated chocolate, decorate with sprigs of fresh mint and serve.

cranberry sunrise

Pink, light and fruity, this refreshing slush is simply delicious and very easy to prepare.

SERVES 2

300 ml/10 fl oz cranberry juice
100 ml/3¹/₂ fl oz orange juice
150 g/5¹/₂ oz fresh raspberries
1 tbsp lemon juice

DECORATION
slices and spirals of fresh lemon or orange

Pour the cranberry juice and orange juice into a food processor and process gently until combined. Add the raspberries and lemon juice and process until a slushy consistency has been reached.

Pour the mixture into glasses and decorate with slices and spirals of fresh lemon or orange.

Serve at once.

ginger fizz

This is a **cool, refreshing slush** for a **hot** day.
It's also very simple to make in a blender.

SERVES 2

350 ml/12fl oz ginger ale
3 sprigs of fresh mint
5 crushed ice cubes

DECORATION
fresh raspberries and mint

Pour the ginger ale into a blender and add the fresh mint. Process until combined.

Strain into chilled tall glasses, two-thirds filled with ice.

Dress with a few raspberries and a sprig of fresh mint.

melon & pineapple crush

When you are feeling jaded, this glorious pairing of sweet and tart flavours will perk you up and give you a boost.

SERVES 2

100 ml/3½ fl oz pineapple juice
4 tbsp orange juice
125 g/4½ oz galia melon,
cut into chunks
140 g/5 oz frozen pineapple chunks
4 ice cubes

DECORATION
slices of galia melon
slices of orange

Pour the pineapple juice and orange juice into a food processor and process gently until combined.

Add the melon, pineapple chunks and ice cubes and process until a slushy consistency has been reached.

Pour the mixture into glasses and decorate with slices of melon and orange.

Serve at once.

strawberries & cream

This becomes **thick** and **icy**, almost like a **sorbet** or **slush**, so don't leave it sitting around to melt.

SERVES 2

60 ml/3 fl oz grapefruit juice, chilled
60 ml/3 fl oz double cream
8–9 large strawberries, hulled (save 2 to serve)
crushed ice

Place all the ingredients into a food processor and blend until a slushy consistency is reached.

Pour into chilled cocktail glasses and finish with the remaining strawberries.

kiwi passion

You can only make this at the last minute and serve it almost **frozen**. Strain to remove the **black seeds** if they worry you!

SERVES 2

2 ripe kiwis, peeled and crushed
150ml/5 fl oz lemonade
juice of 2 passion fruits
splash of lime juice
crushed ice

Put the kiwi, crushed ice and passion fruit juice into a food processor and blend until a slushy consistency has been reached.

Pour the mixture into tall chilled glasses and top up with lemonade.

coconut islander

This can be very **rich**, so **enjoy** in small quantities or dilute a little with **soda water**.

Cut the tops off the pineapples and remove the flesh.

Put all the ingredients into a food processor with the removed pineapple flesh and ice and blend until a slushy consistency is reached.

Pour the slush into the pineapple shells, dress with the cherries or the pineapple leaves and drink through straws.

SERVES 2

2 pineapples
125 ml/4 fl oz pineapple juice
4 tbsp coconut milk
125 ml/4 fl oz milk
4 tbsp crushed pineapple
6 tbsp flaked coconut

DECORATION
ice
cherries

lemon slush

A refreshing summer **fizz** to enjoy with no effort – keep some in the refrigerator ready to **fizz** up at the last minute.

SERVES 2

4 fresh lemons
peel of 1 lemon
2 tbsp sugar
125ml/4 fl oz of lemonade, iced
crushed ice

Squeeze the fresh lemons and pour the juice into chilled glasses filled with crushed ice.

Add the piece of peel and sugar to taste and stir briefly. Add lemonade to taste.

berry slush

Pure fruit blended to a perfectly smooth slush but with no wicked cream added! So enjoy some luxury, knowing it is also very healthy.

SERVES 2

350ml/12 fl oz orange juice
1 banana, sliced and frozen
1lb/450g frozen forest fruits
(such as blueberries, raspberries and
blackberries)

DECORATION
slices of fresh strawberries

Pour the orange juice into a food processor.

Add the banana and half of the forest fruits and process until smooth.

Add the remaining forest fruits and process until smooth.

Pour the mixture into tall glasses and decorate the rims with slices of fresh strawberry.

Add straws and serve.

melon & ginger crush

A really refreshing summer drink, this melon crush is quick and simple to make. If you can't buy kaffir limes, ordinary limes are fine.

SERVES 2

1 small melon
3 tbsp ginger wine
2 tbsp kaffir lime juice
crushed ice
1 lime

Peel, deseed and coarsely chop the melon flesh.

Place in a blender or food processor with the ginger wine and lime juice and blend on high speed until the mixture is smooth.

Place plenty of crushed ice in 2 medium straight-sided glasses and pour the melon and ginger crush over the ice.

Cut the lime into thin slices, cut a slit in four of them, and slip one on to the side of each glass. Add the remaining slices of lime to each glass.

merry berry

Cranberries make wonderfully colourful and tasty drinks. This **vibrant slush** not only looks good, but tastes **delicious** too.

SERVES 2

350 g/12 oz cranberries, thawed if frozen
425 ml/15 fl oz cranberry juice, chilled
300 ml/10 fl oz natural yogurt
2–3 tbsp clear honey

Place the berries and juice in the blender and process until smooth. Add the yogurt and the honey and process again until combined.

Taste and add more honey if necessary.

Pour into chilled glasses and serve.

sparkling peach melba

This simple but perfect partnership of peaches and raspberries is a classic combination and makes a wonderful slush.

SERVES 2

3¹/₂ oz/90g raspberries, puréed
250ml/8 fl oz peach juice
crushed ice
250ml/8oz sparkling water

Sieve the raspberry purée and blend with the peach juice and crushed ice until all ingredients are combined.

Pour the slush into tall tumblers and top up with sparkling water.

Stir gently.

carrot & orange cream

This drink looks and tastes **fabulous** but also contains plenty of health-giving carotene and vitamin C.

SERVES 2

175 ml/6 fl oz carrot juice
175 ml/6 fl oz orange juice
150 g/5¹/₂ oz vanilla ice cream
6 ice cubes

DECORATION
slices of orange
strips of orange peel

Pour the carrot juice and orange juice into a food processor and process gently until well combined. Add the ice cream and process until thoroughly blended.

Add the ice and process until smooth. Pour the mixture into glasses, decorate with slices of orange and strips of orange peel and serve.

melon & ginger slush

Melon and ginger combine to make a very healthy and refreshing summer slush.

SERVES 2

1 ripe melon, peeled, deseeded and
cut into chunks
juice of 2 limes
1 tbsp grated fresh root ginger
4 tbsp unrefined caster sugar
1 egg white, lightly whisked
fresh strawberries or raspberries,
to serve

Put the melon, lime juice and ginger into a food processor or blender and process until smooth. Pour into a measuring jug and make up to 600 ml/1 pint with cold water.

Pour into a bowl and stir in the sugar. Beat in the egg white.

Transfer to a freezerproof container and freeze until a slushy consistency is reached.

Serve with strawberries or raspberries.

peppermint ice

This luxury **drink** can vary in colour – you may prefer **mint chocolate chip ice cream** and find it is almost white. You could add a few drops of colouring to make it brighter.

SERVES 2

150ml/5 fl oz milk
2 tbsp peppermint syrup
14oz/400g peppermint ice cream
sprigs of fresh mint

Pour the milk and peppermint syrup into a food processor and process gently until combined.

Add the peppermint ice cream and process until smooth.

Pour the mixture into iced glasses and decorate with sprigs of fresh mint.

Add straws and serve.

berry berry red

This **combination** is delicious with fresh or frozen **raspberries**, so you can make it all year round. Cut down on the **meringue** if you find it too sweet a finish.

SERVES 2

2 oz/50g raspberries
150ml/5 fl oz cranberry and raspberry juice
150ml/5 fl oz blackberry-flavoured sparkling water
1 small meringue, crumbled
crushed ice

Blend the raspberries with the juice and crushed ice until all ingredients are combined.

Place half the meringue in the base of a tall glass, pour on the fruit slush and top up with the sparkling water.

Decorate with raspberries and the remaining crumbled meringue.

blueberry & raspberry slush

Berries release their sugars very slowly, so this drink is the perfect pick-me-up when you need an energy boost.

SERVES 2

40g/2 oz blueberries
100 g/4 oz raspberries,
thawed if frozen
1 tsp clear honey
300ml/10 fl oz live or bio yogurt
1 heaped tbsp crushed ice
1 tbsp sesame seeds

Place the blueberries into a food processor and blend until a slushy consistency is reached.

Add the raspberries, honey and yogurt and process for a further minute.

Add the ice and sesame seeds and process again for a further minute.

Pour into tall glasses and serve immediately.

smooth & creamy

luxurious and tempting, these delicious drinks offer a true tonic to the bustle of everyday life. Treat yourself to a feast of silky shakes, including a buttermilkshake and a damson dream.

coffee banana cooler

A powerhouse for those who lead an active life – this milkshake tastes fabulous too.

SERVES 2

300 ml/10 fl oz milk
4 tbsp instant coffee powder
150 g/5½ oz vanilla ice cream
2 bananas, sliced and frozen

Pour the milk into a food processor, add the coffee powder and process gently until combined. Add half of the vanilla ice cream and process gently, then add the remaining ice cream and process until well combined.

When the mixture is thoroughly blended, add the bananas and process until smooth.

Pour the mixture into glasses and serve.

raspberry ripple rice cream

A fresh-tasting, **non-dairy shake** with **no** animal products, **no cholesterol, no lactose** and no problem! Rice 'milk' should be **kept cold** in the fridge for the **best-tasting results**. Soya milk can be used instead, but the rice 'milk' tastes much nicer.

SERVES 2

125 g/4¹/₂ oz frozen raspberries
300 ml/10 fl oz rice 'milk'
or soya milk

Put the raspberries and half the rice 'milk' into a food processor and process until smooth.

Strain into a jug and carefully stir through the remaining rice 'milk' to give a marbled effect.

Pour into glasses and serve still very cold.

peppermint refresher

Surprisingly both hot and cold on the tongue, this minty cooler will restore vitality and vigour.

SERVES 2

150 ml/5 fl oz milk
2 tbsp peppermint syrup
400 g/14 oz peppermint ice cream

DECORATION
sprigs of fresh mint

Pour the milk and peppermint syrup into a food processor and process gently until combined.

Add the peppermint ice cream and process until smooth.

Pour the mixture into tall glasses and decorate with sprigs of fresh mint.

Add straws and serve.

creamy maple shake

Maple, vanilla and almond are delicate flavours that complement each other perfectly.

SERVES 2

150 ml/5 fl oz milk
2 tbsp maple syrup
400 g/14 oz vanilla ice cream
1 tbsp almond essence

DECORATION
chopped almonds

Pour the milk and maple syrup into a food processor and process gently until combined.

Add the ice cream and almond essence and process until smooth.

Pour the mixture into glasses and scatter the chopped nuts over the shakes.

Add straws and serve.

mocha cream

The heavenly pairing of **coffee** and **chocolate** can be improved only by the addition of whipped cream.

SERVES 2

200 ml/7 fl oz milk
50 ml/2 fl oz single cream
1 tbsp brown sugar
2 tbsp cocoa powder
1 tbsp coffee syrup or instant coffee powder
6 ice cubes

DECORATION
whipped cream
grated chocolate

Put the milk, cream and sugar into a food processor and process gently until combined.

Add the cocoa powder and coffee syrup or powder and process well, then add the ice cubes and process until smooth.

Pour the mixture into glasses. Top with whipped cream, scatter the grated chocolate over the drinks and serve.

strawberries & cream milkshake

The ultimate strawberry milkshake! Forget about synthetic strawberry-flavoured syrups – this is the real thing: a gorgeous flavour and fantastically fruity. Set off the pale colouring with some pretty green mint leaves.

SERVES 2

150 g/5½ oz frozen strawberries
100 ml/3½ fl oz single cream
200 ml/7 fl oz cold full-cream milk
1 tbsp caster sugar

DECORATION
mint leaves

Put the strawberries, cream, milk and caster sugar into a food processor and process until smooth.

Pour into glasses and serve decorated with mint leaves.

guava goodness

Guavas are remarkably high in vitamin C, and, when blended with milk, provide a very nutritious start to any day.

SERVES 2

400 g/14 oz canned guavas, drained
250 ml/9 fl oz ice-cold milk

cereal bars, to serve

Place the guavas into a food processor and pour in the milk. Process until well blended.

Strain into glasses to remove the hard seeds. Serve with a cereal bar if liked.

peach bliss

Different fruits combine with peaches to make one marvellously fruity drink.

SERVES 2

175 ml/6 fl oz milk
225 g/8 oz canned
peach slices, drained
2 fresh apricots, chopped
400 g/14 oz fresh strawberries, hulled
and sliced
2 bananas, sliced and frozen

DECORATION
slices of strawberry

Pour the milk into a food processor. Add the peach slices and process gently until combined. Add the apricots and process gently until combined.

Add the strawberries and banana slices and process until smooth.

Pour the mixture into glasses and decorate the rims with fresh strawberries.

Serve at once.

chocolate milkshake

The ultimate milkshake for children and chocoholics alike, this drink is supremely satisfying.

SERVES 2

150 ml/5 fl oz milk
2 tbsp chocolate syrup
400 g/14 oz chocolate ice cream

DECORATION
grated chocolate

Pour the milk and chocolate syrup into a food processor and process gently until combined.

Add the chocolate ice cream and process until smooth. Pour the mixture into tall glasses and scatter the grated chocolate over the shakes.

Serve at once.

lassi

Traditionally served as an accompaniment to a hot Indian curry, lassi makes the perfect cooler.

SERVES 2

100 ml/3^1/$_2$ fl oz natural yogurt
500 ml/18 fl oz milk
1 tbsp rose water
3 tbsp honey
1 ripe mango, stoned and diced
6 ice cubes

DECORATION
edible rose petals, optional

Pour the yogurt and milk into a food processor and process gently until combined.

Add the rose water and honey and process until thoroughly blended, then add the mango along with the ice cubes and process until smooth.

Pour the mixture into glasses, decorate with edible rose petals, if using, and serve.

almond milk

Nuts are little powerhouses of energy, so this drink is the perfect way to restore energy.

SERVES 2

25 g/1 oz blanched almonds
300 ml/10 fl oz milk, chilled
125 ml/4 fl oz natural yogurt
2 tbsp caster sugar

Dry-fry the almonds in a heavy based frying pan, tossing and turning frequently, for 30–60 seconds or until golden. Remove from the heat and allow to cool.

Place the cooled nuts into a blender and process until finely chopped. Add the milk, yogurt and sugar and process until smooth.

Pour into chilled glasses and serve.

spiced banana milkshake

This is a Caribbean combination of fruit and spices that will tantalise the tastebuds.

SERVES 2

300 ml/10 fl oz milk
1/2 tsp mixed spice
150 g/5 1/2 oz banana ice cream
2 bananas, sliced and frozen

Pour the milk into a food processor and add the mixed spice. Add half of the banana ice cream and process gently until combined, then add the remaining ice cream and process until well blended.

When the mixture is well combined, add the bananas and process until smooth.

Pour the mixture into tall glasses. Add straws and serve at once.

apricot & almond milk

Almond milk is used around the Mediterranean and is best made with new season's nuts. It is fiddly to blanch and peel almonds, but the extra flavour is worth it. You can use ready-blanched nuts but not ground or flaked almonds.

SERVES 2

150 g/5½ oz fresh almonds
300 ml/10 fl oz boiling water, plus water for scalding
200 g /7 oz ripe apricots
2 tsp demerara sugar

Pour some boiling water over the almonds to scald them. Drain them and, as soon as the nuts are cool enough to handle, slip off the brown skins and put the kernels into the food processor with 150 ml/5 fl boiling water. Grind the nuts and water in the food processor, then add a further 150 ml/5 fl oz water and process again. Strain through a sieve and allow to cool. Rinse out the food processor.

Pour boiling water over the apricots to scald them. Drain, then peel and quarter them, discarding the stones. Put them in the food processor and purée. Combine the almond milk and the apricot purée in the food processor and process until blended.

Pour into glasses and top with a crunchy layer of demerara sugar.

tropical storm

Revive yourself with this invigorating and exuberant tropical shake.

SERVES 2

250 ml/9 fl oz milk
50 ml/2 fl oz coconut milk
150 g/5½ oz vanilla ice cream
2 bananas, sliced and frozen
200 g/7 oz canned pineapple chunks, drained
1 papaya, deseeded and diced

DECORATION
grated fresh coconut
wedges of fresh pineapple

Pour the milk and coconut milk into a food processor and process gently until combined. Add half of the ice cream and process gently, then add the remaining ice cream and process until smooth.

Add the bananas and process well, then add the pineapple chunks and papaya and process until smooth.

Pour the mixture into tall glasses. Scatter the grated coconut over the shakes and decorate the rims with pineapple wedges.

Serve at once.

peach & orange milkshake

A luscious combination of fruits to leave you restored, revived and refreshed.

SERVES 2

100 ml/3½ fl oz milk
125 ml/4 fl oz peach yogurt
100 ml/3½ fl oz orange juice
225 g/8 oz canned
peach slices, drained
6 ice cubes

DECORATION
strips of orange peel

Pour the milk, yogurt and orange juice into a food processor and process gently until combined.

Add the peach slices and ice cubes and process until smooth. Pour the mixture into glasses and decorate with strips of orange peel.

Add straws and serve.

kiwi & lime shake

This drink provides a good source of vitamin C, as well as a wonderfully refreshing sweet and sharp flavour.

SERVES 2

150 ml/5 fl oz milk
juice of 2 limes
2 kiwi fruit, chopped
1 tbsp sugar
400 g/14 oz vanilla ice cream

DECORATION
slices of kiwi fruit
strips of lime peel

Pour the milk and lime juice into a food processor and process gently until combined.

Add the kiwi fruit and sugar and process gently, then add the ice cream and process until smooth.

Pour the mixture into glasses and decorate with slices of kiwi fruit and strips of lime peel.

Serve at once.

buttermilkshake

Although it tastes **deliciously rich**, cultured buttermilk is low in fat and makes a **lovely creamy** milkshake. The buttermilk is combined with **strawberries** here, but you can substitute any other soft fruit.

SERVES 2

120 g/4½ oz frozen strawberries
300 ml/10 fl oz cultured buttermilk
½ tsp vanilla essence
2 tbsp caster sugar

DECORATION
strawberry slices

Put the strawberries, buttermilk, vanilla essence and caster sugar into a food processor and process until smooth.

Decorate the rims of the glasses with strawberry slices. Serve at once with straws.

black cherry bliss

Chocolate and cherries are a classic combination. You can also serve this as a **dessert**, with a couple of dark chocolate thins.

SERVES 2

150 g/5½ oz black cherries
3 large scoops of luxury
white chocolate ice cream
150 ml/5 fl oz milk

Halve and stone the black cherries. Put these into a food processor and process until puréed.

Add the ice cream and milk and process briefly to mix well.

Pour into glasses, adding long-handled spoons.

almond & banana shake

A smooth and velvety shake which tastes delicious. The almonds used can also aid in reducing cholesterol.

SERVES 2

50g/2 oz whole blanched almonds
300 ml/10 fl oz milk
1 ripe banana, halved
½ tsp natural vanilla extract
ground cinnamon, for sprinkling

Put the almonds into a food processor and process until very finely chopped.

Add the milk, bananas and vanilla extract and blend until smooth and creamy.

Pour into glasses and sprinkle with cinnamon.

plum fluff

You will need **perfectly ripe plums** for this fabulously frothy, **fruity recipe**. Dark ones – such as Marjorie's Seedling – give a better colour.

SERVES 2

4 medium ripe plums, stoned
200 ml/7 fl oz ice-cold milk
2 scoops of luxury vanilla ice cream

crumbly oat biscuits, to serve

Put the plums, milk and ice cream into a food processor and process until smooth and frothy.

Pour into glasses and serve at once with crumbly oat biscuits.

damson dream

A deep, rich and fruity shake for the end of the summer.

SERVES 2

250 g/9 oz ripe damsons
200 ml/7 fl oz water
1 tbsp golden granulated sugar
4 scoops of frozen yogurt (plain)
or ice cream
2 Italian almond or
pistachio biscotti, crumbled

extra biscotti, crumbled,
to serve

Put the damsons, water and sugar into a small saucepan. Cover tightly and simmer for about 15 minutes, until the damsons have split and are very soft. Allow to cool.

Strain off the liquid into a food processor and add the frozen yogurt or ice cream. Process until smooth and frothy.

Pour into glasses and sprinkle with the crumbled biscotti. Serve with extra biscotti on the side.

smooth nectarine shake

Mango and nectarine is an inspired combination of fruits, made all the more special with the clever addition of lemon sorbet.

SERVES 2

250 ml/9 fl oz milk
350 g/12 oz lemon sorbet
1 ripe mango, stoned and diced
2 ripe nectarines, stoned and diced

Pour the milk into a food processor, add half of the lemon sorbet and process gently until combined. Add the remaining sorbet and process until smooth.

When the mixture is thoroughly blended, gradually add the mango and nectarines and process until smooth.

Pour the mixture into glasses, add straws and serve.

Index